D1634125

In case of loss, please return to:

_____

_____

_____

_____

As a reward: $ _____

MICHAEL GRAVES

Inspiration and Process in Architecture

Edited by
Francesca Serrazanetti, Matteo Schubert

Published by Moleskine SpA

Series and Book Editors
Francesca Serrazanetti, Matteo Schubert

Publishing Coordinator
Igor Salmi

Graphic design
A+G AchilliGhizzardiAssociati

ISBN 978-88-6732-692-1

Text "Architecture and the lost art of drawing"
by Michael Graves

First edition October 2014
Printed by Dongguan Tai Fai in China

We would like to thank
Michael Graves, FAIA
Karen Nichols, FAIA
Dounia Tamri-Loeper
Mary Kate Murray

Inspiration and Process in Architecture is a series of monographs on key figures in modern and contemporary architecture. It offers a reading of the practice of design which emphasises the value of freehand drawing as part of the creative process. Each volume provides a different perspective, revealing secrets and insights and showing the various observation techniques languages, characters, forms and means of communication.

Contents

5   Writings
6   Architecture and the lost art of drawing
10   Interview with Michael Graves

15   Drawings
16   Drawing Lessons from Rome
38   Referential Sketches: A Visual Diary
84   Preparatory Studies: Tangible Speculation
102   Telling Stories: Character and Context
130   Imagined Landscapes

139   Biography

Engineering Research Center
University of Cincinnati
Cincinnati, Ohio
Entrance façade study
Ink on paper, 1990

Writings

Architecture and the lost art of drawing

By Michael Graves

It has become fashionable in many architectural circles to declare the death of drawing. What has happened to our profession, and our art, to cause the supposed end of our most powerful means of conceptualizing and representing architecture?

The computer, of course. With its tremendous ability to organize and present data, the computer is transforming every aspect of how architects work, from sketching their first impressions of an idea to creating complex construction documents for contractors. For centuries, the noun "digit" (from the Latin "digitus") has been defined as "finger", but now its adjectival form, "digital", relates to data. Are our hands becoming obsolete as creative tools? Are they being replaced by machines? And where does that leave the architectural creative process?

Today architects typically use computer-aided design software with names like AutoCAD and Revit, a tool for "building information modeling". Buildings are no longer just designed visually and spatially; they are "computed" via interconnected databases.

I've been practicing architecture since 1964, and my office is not immune. Like most architects, we routinely use these and other software programs, especially for construction documents, but also for developing designs and making presentations. There's nothing inherently problematic about that, as long as it's not just that.

Architecture cannot divorce itself from drawing, no matter how impressive the technology gets. Drawings are not just end products: they are part of the thought process of architectural design. Drawings express the interaction of our minds, eyes and hands. This last statement is absolutely crucial to the difference between those who draw to conceptualize architecture and those who use the computer.

Of course, in some sense drawing can't be dead: there is a vast market for the original work of respected architects. I have had several one-man shows in galleries and museums in New York and elsewhere, and my drawings can be found in the collections of the Metropolitan Museum of Art, the Museum of Modern Art and the Cooper-Hewitt.

But can the value of drawings be simply that of a collector's artifact or a pretty picture? No. I have a real purpose in making each drawing, either to remember something or to study something. Each one is part of a process and not an end in itself. I'm personally fascinated not just by what architects choose to draw but also by what they choose not to draw.

For decades I have argued that architectural drawing can be divided into three types, which I call the "referential sketch", the "preparatory study" and the "definitive drawing". The definitive drawing, the final and most developed of the three, is almost universally produced on the computer nowadays, and that is appropriate. But what about the other two? What is their value in the creative process? What can they teach us?

The referential sketch serves as a visual diary, a record of an architect's discovery. It can be as simple as a shorthand notation of a design concept or can describe details of a larger composition. It might not even be a drawing that relates to a building or any time in history. It's not likely to represent "reality", but rather to capture an idea.

These sketches are thus inherently fragmentary and selective. When I draw something, I remember it. The drawing is a reminder of the idea that caused me to record it in the first place. That visceral connection, that thought process, cannot be replicated by a computer.

The second type of drawing, the preparatory study, is typically part of a progression of drawings that elaborate a design. Like the referential sketch, it may not reflect a linear process. (I find computer-aided design much more linear.) I personally like to draw on translucent yellow tracing paper, which allows me to layer one drawing on top of another, building on what I've drawn before and, again, creating a personal, emotional connection with the work.

With both of these types of drawings, there is a certain joy in their creation, which comes from the interaction between the mind and the hand. Our physical and mental interactions with drawings are formative acts. In a handmade drawing, whether on an electronic tablet or on paper, there are intonations, traces of intentions and speculation. This is not unlike the way a musician might intone a note or how a riff in jazz would be understood subliminally and put a smile on your face.

I find this quite different from today's "parametric design", which allows the computer to generate form from a set of instructions, sometimes resulting in so-called blob architecture. The designs are complex and interesting in their own way, but they lack the emotional content of a design derived from hand.

Years ago I was sitting in a rather boring faculty meeting at Princeton. To pass the time, I pulled out my pad to start drawing a plan, probably of some building I was designing. An equally bored colleague was watching me, amused. I came to a point of indecision and passed the pad to him. He added a few lines and passed it back.

The game was on. Back and forth we went, drawing five lines each, then four and so on.

While we didn't speak, we were engaged in a dialogue over this plan and we understood each other perfectly. I suppose that you could have a debate like that with words, but it would have been entirely different. Our game was not about winners or losers, but about a shared language. We had a genuine love for making this drawing. There was an insistence, by the act of drawing, that the composition would stay open, that the speculation would stay "wet" in the sense of a painting. Our plan was without scale and we could as easily have been drawing a domestic building as a portion of a city. It was the act of drawing that allowed us to speculate.

As I work with my computer-savvy students and staff today, I notice that something is lost when they draw only on the computer. It is analogous to hearing the words of a novel read aloud, when reading them on paper allows us to daydream a little, to make associations beyond the literal sentences on the page. Similarly, drawing by hand stimulates the imagination and allows us to speculate about ideas, a good sign that we're truly alive.

Originally published in "The New York Times", September 1, 2012

Interview with Michael Graves

6 6 *The two years spent at the American Academy in Rome, your travels in Italy and Europe, the days spent out of the studio to draw ancient architecture, have profoundly influenced your work. Before you, hundreds of great architects of the past have found and developed their own design trajectory after completing travels in Italy and Europe, being inspired from the analysis of what they had observed. In the era of "Google earth" and "Instagram", does it still make sense, for an architect, a trip with pen and paper in hand?*

It absolutely makes sense, even though some, unlike me, prefer their computers and cameras. When I draw, especially when travelling, it is with a purpose, to document something specific that I want to remember. A drawing is not all-inclusive in the way that a photograph might be. I often say that what you choose not to draw is as important as what you draw. There is a subliminal connection made between the hand and the mind. It's like writing a note to yourself in visual form. The drawing triggers recollection of what you saw and why it had meaning to you at the time. I think that's partly why, for many architects, travelling and recording what they've seen becomes formative to future design work.

6 6 *The drawings published in the book seem to be a "collection" of references, that you register and then select, using them as an abacus of forms. The composition of your architecture seems to be the result of the juxtaposition of these individual elements: simple shapes, parts of classic architecture, archetypes. Is there a direct connection between the recording of the existing and its "reuse" for the project?*

No, typically there's little direct connection between a referential sketch and an eventual building project. However, as I mentioned, an individual sketch is often just a fragment, a notation of an idea, and the idea might become part of a larger work. I often create compositions that I call "archaic landscapes" in which small, archetypal forms are arrayed within landscape fields. Some of these are incorporated into buildings more directly, as pavilions.

66 *In your "referential sketches" there is a parallel between details of objects or sculptures and architecture, as if there was a search for a connection between them. Could you tell us about your process of analysis and synthesis of this particular way to "register" the elements at different scales?*

Whether I am drawing a teacup or a building, I am always working out the composition, which to me means the proportions of individual elements and their scalar relationship to other elements. People often confuse scale and size. To draw a large object is not so different from drawing a small object except in complexity.

66 *In the drawings of your architectural projects, the different elements seem to be composed by following a process of assembly that creates a sort of complex "still life", where the environment is secondary. What is the relation between the architecture and the landscape around it? Are your drawings also an abstraction of reality, an attempt to trace out new archetypes universally possible?*

I have always been fascinated by the relationships among the parts of a building, making a hierarchical and therefore legible composition that, by its nature, is intuitive to understand and navigate. The same is true of the relationships among buildings as they define the open space that makes up the public realm of a city, or even a campus. The figure-ground drawings of the plans of Rome created by Giambattista Nolli in 1748 profile the public space of the city, making the outdoor spaces of streets and piazzas continuous with the interior rooms of public buildings. As a result, you start to understand the reciprocity between buildings and open space. Corollary to that, we see how the facades of buildings and smaller scale elements such as porticos and pergolas start to define the open spaces as public "rooms", whether they are built spaces such as courtyards or landscaped spaces such as gardens.

As for your question about new archetypes, I do think about universally understood archetypes and models. While they evolve and become transformed, I don't strive for "new", just for the sake of newness. "New", after all, eventually becomes old.

❝ *In a few paintings published in this volume there is the presence of an easel with a canvas: it seems to be a sort of "moderator" between the observer and the architectural landscape. Looking closely at what is represented within the canvas then, one gets the impression that you wanted to represent the analytical process and the synthesis that followed. Is this correct? How would you describe these paintings and the related process?*

I use the easel as a device to create a story within a story, to isolate and emphasize one subject within the larger composition. For example, in the composition that I call "Easel Landscape", the easel holds a book with a painting on the cover. The painting represents a folly that I designed, which incorporates archetypal, geometric forms in a rather abstract relationship with each other. On the hills beyond are buildings that incorporate some of those archetypal forms. I am thereby showing the origins of some of the ideas.

In the print made from a painting of the scaffolding of the Washington Monument while it was being restored, the easel holds an image of the Monument before the scaffolding was erected, or perhaps the finished monument after its restoration.

❝ *During your career, which has spanned part of the twentieth century and seen a great revolution in the use of drawing, can you find fundamental stages? Are there any writings/books on this subject that you consider as cornerstones, which an architect can not do without in his training?*

As a child, I became interested in being an architect because I was interested in drawing and had an aptitude for it. Of course, since there were no computers then, my schooling and early training was entirely based on hand-drawing. When I won the Rome Prize and spent two years at the American Academy in Rome, I became very serious about documenting what I saw through drawings. In the 1980s, architects' drawings were prized and widely exhibited for themselves as well as for their indication of design ideas and processes. As computer technology became more and more prevalent, it took over for hand drawing in producing documents used to build buildings, and that was expedient and appropriate. However, I think something was lost when computers started to be used to generate the compositions, to develop the ideas. That trend seems to be reversing itself in recent years, when more and more architects recognize the value of both hand drawings and computer drawings.

When I was in Rome in the early 1960s, in addition to drawing and documenting architecture, I became acquainted with architectural "literature", books that include drawings, which I now regard as essential to an architect's education. I often refer to Palladio's Four Books as they record and emphasize elements of architecture that he thought to be paramount. I look at volumes by Durand and Letarouilly, as they teach us so much about the making of plans. I am also interested how much an architect like Piranesi can teach us about the method and construction of ancient buildings.

66 *Over the years you have written essays and articles about hand-drawing, reminding the importance of this tool in the genesis of the project. Looking around, can you still find any hope for the survival of "the lost art of drawing"? And do you think it needs to be reinvented or re-founded in order to be a suitable tool in the contemporary world?*

Even though the article that introduces this volume refers to drawing as a "lost art", I think that's simply how some today regard it since they are so dependent on the computer. You would be surprised at how many architects conceptualize their buildings through hand-drawing, even when the building compositions are eventually developed in the computer. Computer drawings and hand drawing are both useful. I will always draw by hand not only because I love to, but also because it's essential to how I think and create. For me, the relationship between the hand and the eye that evolves through drawing is intrinsically an act of the mind and becomes a creative act in the conceptualization of our physical world and the objects within it.

**Ikon fruit bowl for
Waechterbacher Keramik**
Ink on paper, 1981

Drawings

Drawing Lessons from Rome

Michael Graves was awarded the Prix de Rome in 1960 and spent two years studying at the American Academy in Rome, an experience that would transform how he thought about architecture and how he documented it through drawing. In the tradition of architects who, over centuries, embarked on "Grand Tours" of Italy and Greece, Graves made drawings of buildings that he thought contained valuable lessons. The drawings, at once mnemonic and representational, were also, in his words, "drawn with a purpose and intended to document a characteristic that I wanted to be able to recall".

Many of the drawings from that period are large pen and ink compositions on paper of approximately 41 x 27 inches, which Graves spread on the cobblestone paving in front of buildings and monuments throughout Rome. One of his colleagues at the Academy, the painter Lennart Anderson, remarked that by working on the ground and drawing so expressionistically, Graves denied himself the analytic rigor possible in a more frontal relationship with his subjects. Anderson also suggested a more sparing use of line, reducing the drawing to the essence of what Graves was trying to capture. This exchange led to a series of drawings, mostly in pencil, on cream-colored, clay-coated paper averaging 11 x 14 inches or smaller. In addition to touring Rome and other cities in Italy, Graves visited buildings by Le Corbusier in France, one of the sources of inspiration for his architectural designs.

right
Santa Croce in Gerusalemme
Rome, Italy
Ink on paper, date unknown (1960s)

following page
Basilica of Maxentius
Rome, Italy
Ink on paper, 1960

19

above
Santa Chiara
Bra, Italy
Pencil on paper, 1962

left
Santo Nome di Maria
Rome, Italy
Ink on paper, 1961

Fontana dell'Acqua Paola
Rome, Italy
Ink on paper, 1961

Sant'Ivo alla Sapienza
Rome, Italy
Ink on paper, 1961

23

above
Domus Augustana
Rome, Italy
Ink on paper, 1961

left
San Carlino
Rome, Italy
Pen on paper, 1961

Santa Maria delle Carceri, Prato
G. Dance

aboce left
Santa Maria delle Carceri
Prato, Italy
Pencil on paper, 1962

below left
Pazzi Chapel
Florence, Italy
Pencil on paper, 1962

The Campo
Siena, Italy
Pencil on paper, 1962

San Gimignano
Siena Province, Italy
Pencil on paper, date unknown (1960s)

San Bernardino
Urbino, Italy
Pencil on paper, 1962

Sant'Anastasia and Domus Augustana
Rome, Italy
Pencil on paper, date unknown (1960s)

Santa Maria presso San Satiro
Milan, Italy
Pencil on paper, 1962

The Pantheon
Rome, Italy
Pencil on paper, date unknown

Lion Fountain
Rome, Italy
Pencil on paper, date unknown

S. Maria in Cosmedin, Rome
10-61 / Michael Graves

left
Santa Maria in Cosmedin
Rome, Italy
Pencil on paper, 1961

above
Chapel of Notre Dame du Haut
Ronchamp, France
Pencil on paper, 1962

above and right
Convent of Sainte Marie de La Tourette
Near Lyon, France
Pencil on paper, 1962

37

Referential Sketches: A Visual Diary

In 1977, Michael Graves wrote a seminal article on architectural drawing entitled, "The Necessity for Drawing: Tangible Speculation", which was published in the British journal, "Architectural Design". The article characterized three types of architectural drawing: the referential sketch, the preparatory study, and the definitive drawing. The referential sketch is a visual diary, a record of discovery. It is typically fragmentary but may be developed into a more elaborate composition when remembered and combined with other themes.

Graves' sketchbooks are filled with referential sketches. Some simply document buildings or objects, such as a historic monument that he saw in a book, or a federal style chair that he noticed on a trip to Rhode Island. Others have the capacity for metaphorical associations, such as a pyramidal tomb at Parc Monceau in Paris, which can be thought of as a mock mountain in its landscape. Yet others constitute research into buildings or elements that represent the historic or physical context of a particular project, such as historic central American architectural details that relate to the design of the San Juan Capistrano Library.

right
Referential sketches
Ink on paper, 1980

Roma antica di Pirro Ligorio - 1561

Colonne Termini Colonna
Roma

François Leonard Senault

J. J. Lequeu

Barrière du Trône - Paris
Ledoux 1789

Parc Monceau

39

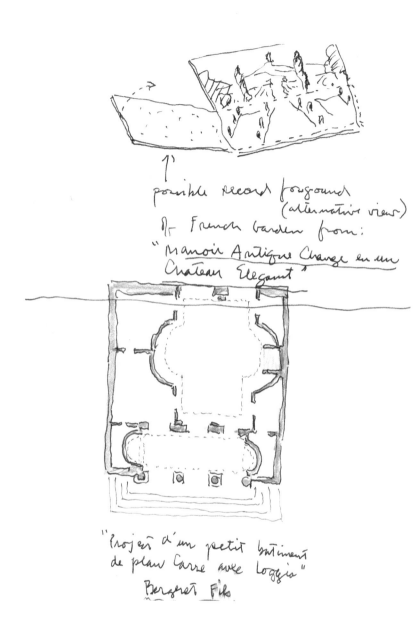

possible second foreground
(alternative views)
of French Garden from:
"Manoir Antique Changé en un
Château Elegant"

"Projet d'un petit bâtiment
de plan Carré avec Loggia"
Bergeret Fils

above (upper)
Alternative views of a French garden
Ink on paper, 1977

above (lower)
Plan of a small building
by Bergeret Fils
Ink and colored pencil on paper, 1977

right
Tower by J. J. Lequeu
Ink and colored pencil on paper, 1977

J. L. Leguen

" L Ile D'Am
et Reponse de
Pecre en lw
en pierre e
la Place de
de la Ville R
et de Camp L
Fortifie de L'E
Gen

Fig 173
pp. 73

Folly in Parc Monceau
Paris, France
Ink and colored pencil on paper, 1977

Parc Monceau
1977

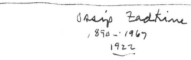

Tower at the Roma Termini Train Station
Rome, Italy
Ink and colored pencil on paper, c. 1977

right
Parti for a Student Project
Ink and colored pencil on paper, c. 1977

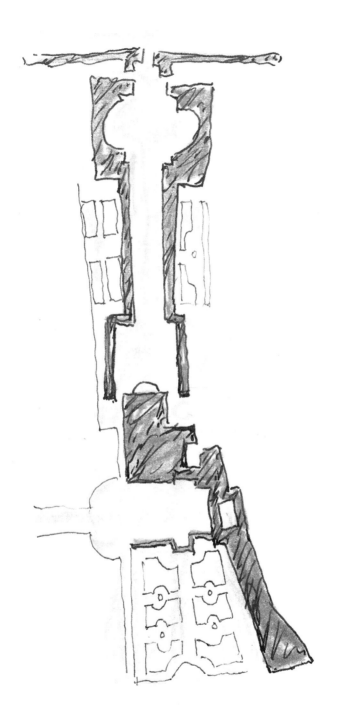

above
Roman Aqueducts in the Campania
Ink on paper, date unknown

below
Castel Sant'Angelo
Rome, Italy
Ink on paper, date unknown

Referential sketch, from Roma
Antica di Stefano du Pérac, 1574
Ink on paper, c. 1976

47

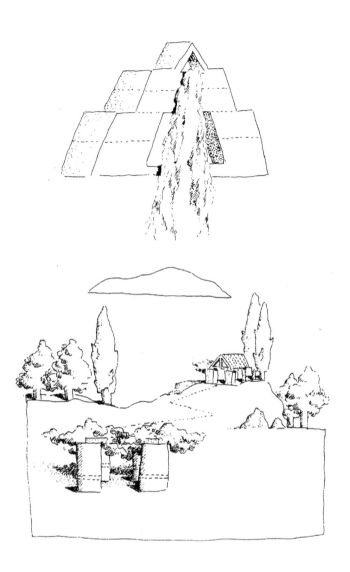

above
Fargo-Moorhead Cultural Center Bridge
Fargo, North Dakota and
Moorhead, Minnesota
Study for the fountain on the bridge
Ink on paper, 1977

below
Sunar Showroom
New York, New York
Referential sketch of pergola
in the landscape
Ink on paper, 1978

variation on
c.... ...en 1756·1845

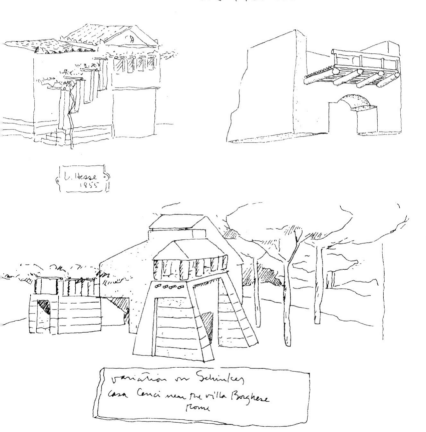

L. Hesse
1855

variation on Schinkel
Casa Cenci near the villa Borghese
Rome

Vacation House
Aspen, Colorado
Referential sketches
Ink on paper, 1978

above
Concept study for a house
1980s

below
Illustration for The Great Gatsby
Sunken Italian garden
Ink on paper, 1985

Illustration for The Great Gatsby
Garden at Gatsby's mansion
Ink on paper, 1985

above
Study for an Outdoor Stage
Pen on paper, date unknown

above
Tomb of Augustus
Ink on paper, date unknown

below
Roman Ruin
Ink on paper, date unknown

Apartment Building in Amsterdam
Pencil on paper, date unknown

Recueil d'Architecture
par Francois bonard ~~Scot~~ Scheult

M. DCCC. XXI

Monument from F.L. Scheult,
Receuil d'Architecture
Ink and colored pencil on paper, 1976

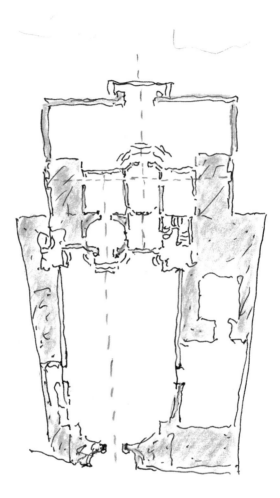

Hotel de Matignon
Rue de Varennes
M. Courtonne
1721
Blondel

above
Plan of Hotel de Matignon
Ink and colored pencil on paper, 1976

right
Penn State Water Tower
Ink on paper, 1976

Penn State
water tower

**Arch at Kew from a painting
by Richard Wilson, 1762**
Ink on paper, 1976

Arch at Kew
painting by Richard Wilson 1762

American Federal Chair
Providence, Rhode Island
Ink on paper, 1977

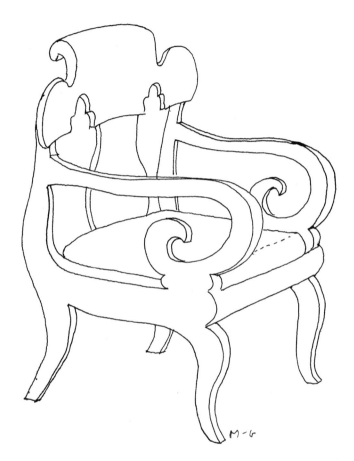

Federas chair c. 1830
American
Providence R.I.
Di Maio
4.3.77

Le Casin de Raphael
from
vue par Ingres

above
Ingres painting, "House of Raphael"
Ink and colored pencil on paper, 1977

right
Raphael painting,
"Disputa del Sacramento"
Ink and colored pencil on paper, 1977

Disputa del Sacramento
from
Raffaello

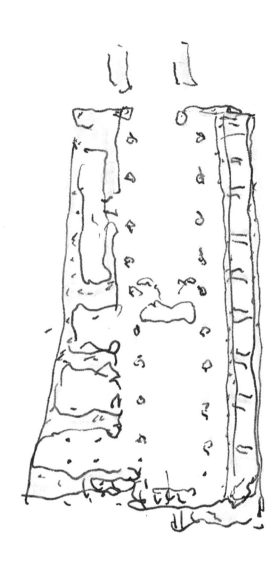

Detail of Roman Forum
Rome, Italy
Ink and colored pencil on paper,
date unknown (1970s)

Folly
Ink on paper, date unknown

Variation on Casa Isolani - Bologna

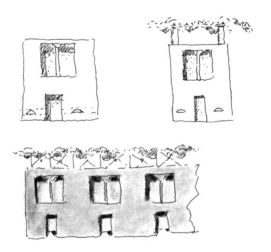

Variations on the Casa Isolani
Bologna, Italy
Ink and colored pencil on paper, c. 1977

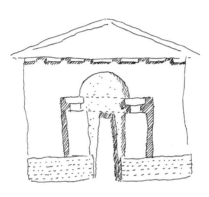

top
**Study for roof pavilion for
The Portland Building**
Ink on Paper, 1979

middle
The Eban family mausoleum, 1798
Ink on paper, date unknown (1980s)

bottom
Giuseppe Rossi, Apartment in Florence
Ink on paper, date unknown (1980s)

Trajan's Market
Ink on Paper, 1978

Rome - Trajan's Market

PYRAMID AT THE CHÂTEAU DE GROUSSAY
IN MONTFORT L'AMAURY

VILLA OF CHARLES
DE BEISTEGUI

EMILIO TERRY
ARCHITECT

above and right
Details of buildings in Guatemala
Referential sketches for the
San Juan Capistrano Library
Ink and colored pencil on paper, 1979

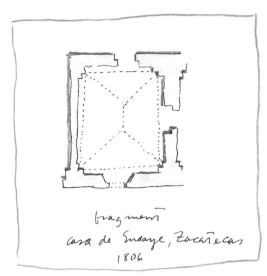

fragment
casa de Ensaye, Zacatecas
1806

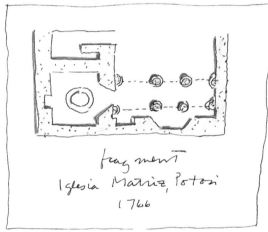

fragment
Iglesia Matriz, Potosi
1766

Actopan
El cerro
La Cantera

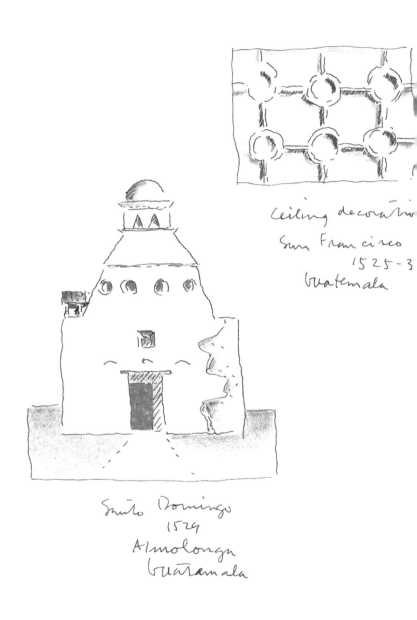

Ceiling decoratio
San Francisco
1525 - 3
Guatemala

Santo Domingo
1529
Almolonga
Guatemala

above and right
Details of buildings in Guatemala
Referential sketches for
the San Juan Capistrano Library
Ink and colored pencil on paper, 1979

Tikas

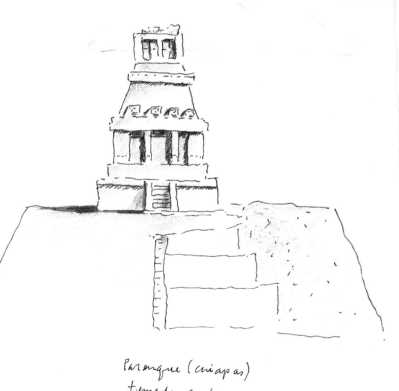

Parangue (chiapas)
temple of the sun

GRAHAMSTOWN, HOUSE ON THE MARKET SQUARE C.1860
SOUTH AFRICA

DESIGN FOR PAVILLION AT STOW 1702 JAMES GIBBS

above
House on the Market Square
Grahamstown. South Africa
Ink on paper, 1981

below
Pavilion at Stow by James Gibbs
Ink on paper, date unknown (1980s)

Prior
the Barn, Exmouth, Devon
1896

Jacques-Louis David

above
above
The "Barn", Exmouth, Devon,
by E.L. Prior
Ink on paper, date unknown (1980s)

below
Portrait of Jacques-Louis David
Ink on paper, date unknown (1980s)

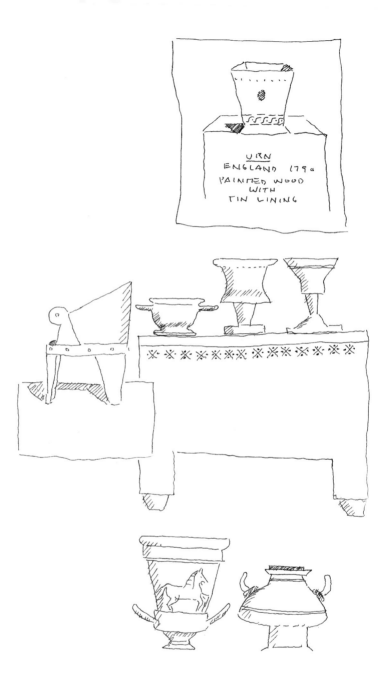

above
Urn, England, 1790
Ink on paper, 1981

below
Urn studies and side chair for Sunar
Ink on paper, 1981

Herbert Baker
House
Johannesburg

cape town
5. 81

above
Herbert Baker House
Johannesburg, South Africa
Ink on paper, 1981

below
Building in Capetown, South Africa
Ink on paper, 1981

Beach in Puerto Rico
Ink on paper, 1981

VIA APPIA

Follies in the Roman Campagna
Ink on paper, date unknown

SAN
GEORGIO
MAJORI

FROM HARRY'S
BAR.
VENICE
APRIL 25 · '82

THE ROMAN THEATRE OF XANTHOS
HARPY-TOMB + SARCOPHAGUS
TOMB

FROM FRANCOIS BOUCHER - LANDSCAPE WITH
A CASTLE AND A MILL   1765

above left
View from Harry's Bar
Venice, Italy
Ink on paper, 1982

below left
Tuscan Landscape
Ink on paper, date unknown (1980s)

above
Tombs at the Roman Theater of Xanthus Turkey
Ink on paper, 1984

below
Landscape with a Castle and a Mill,
after Francois Boucher, 1764
Ink on paper, 1984

Lycean Rock Tomb
Acropolis of Telemessos, Turkey
Ink on paper, 1984

LIGHTHOUSE AT BABA ADASI   II CEN. A.D. ROMAN

CONSTRUCTION TECHNIQUE WITH SCAFFOLDING
USED AT BABA ADASI

above
Lighthouse at Baba Adasi
Turkey
Ink on paper, 1984

below
Construction Technique with Scaffolding
Baba Adasi, Turkey
Ink on paper, 1984

Sarcophagus at Aperlae, Turkey
Ink on paper, 1984

Dovecote at Kas, Turkey
Ink on paper, 1984

DOVECOTE AT KAS TURKEY
6·7·84

Preparatory Studies: Tangible Speculation

In Michael Graves' architectural and product design practices, projects are often initiated as hand-drawings that he refers to as "preparatory studies". The preparatory study, at least in its initial stages, documents the process of inquiry and is deliberately experimental and speculative by nature. Sometimes recorded in sketchbooks and sometimes on translucent tracing paper overlaid on previous drawings, these studies may offer alternative formal approaches or variations on a theme, or may simply document the sequence of ideas leading toward a definitive design.

In architecture, preparatory studies initiate and develop the parti, the central organizing idea, through a series of plan notations and three-dimensional studies. For example, the Plocek House in Warren, New Jersey was conceived as a series of pavilions that would engage the landscape of the sloping site in plan and section. The architecture and the surrounding landscape were shaped into fragments that would create outdoor rooms similar to the figurative nature of the interior plans. The initial sketches of the parti became the framework for the eventual design of the house.

Plocek House
Warren, New Jersey

right Above
Parti sketch, 1977
Ink and colored pencil on paper

right below
Site Plan Study
Ink on paper, 1977

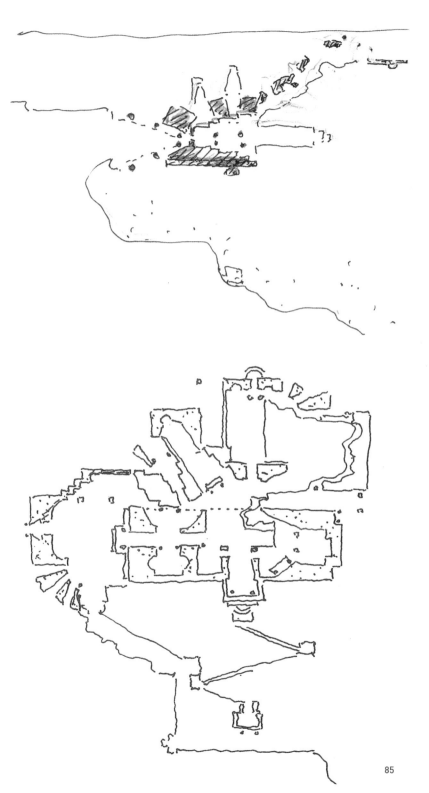

85

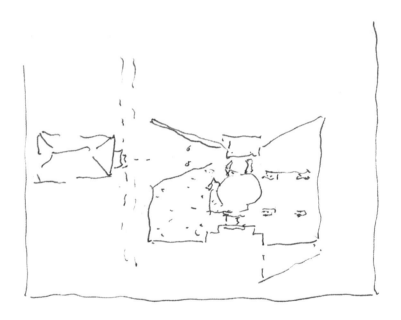

Crooks House
Fort Wayne, Indiana
Parti sketch
ink on paper, 1976

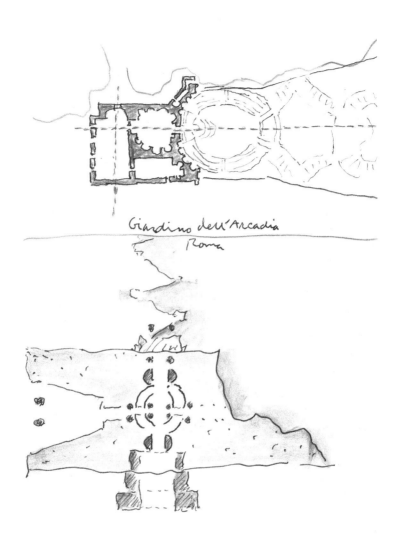

Giardino dell'Arcadia
Roma

above
Parti of the Arcadian Garden
Near the American Academy in Rome
Ink and colored pencil on paper, 1977

below
Plocek House
Warren, New Jersey
Parti study
Ink and colored pencil on paper, 1977

87

Schulman House
Princeton, New Jersey
Plan and massing studies
Ink on paper, 1976

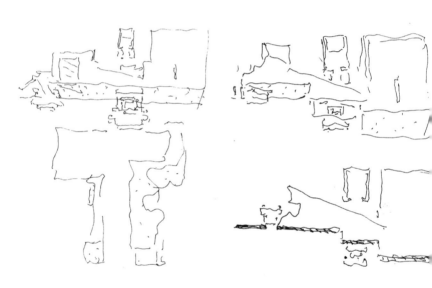

Yacht Club Feasibility Study
Brielle, New Jersey
Parti study
Ink on paper, 1980

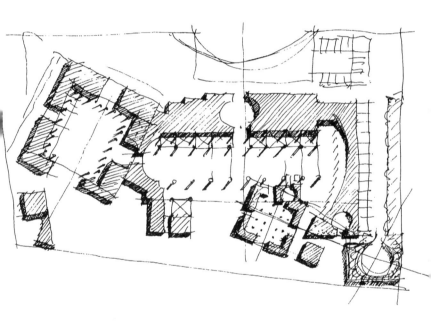

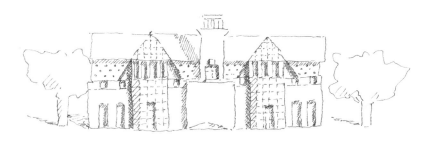

Erickson Alumni Center
West Virginia University
Morgantown, West Virginia

above
Garden façade study
Ink and water color on paper, 1984

below
Garden façade study
Ink on paper, 1984

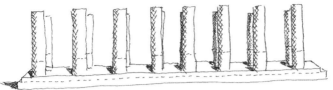

PERGOLA
FOR TEXTILE EXHIB.
MILANO
19 82

INFORMATION
KIOSK

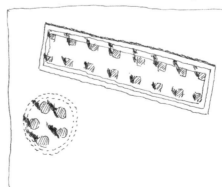

Alcantara Textile Pavilion
Milan, Italy
Studies of plan and pergola
Ink and colored pencil on paper, 1982

Beach House
Loveladies, New Jersey

above
Preliminary façade study
Ink and gouache on paper, 1979

below
Massing study
Ink on paper, 1979

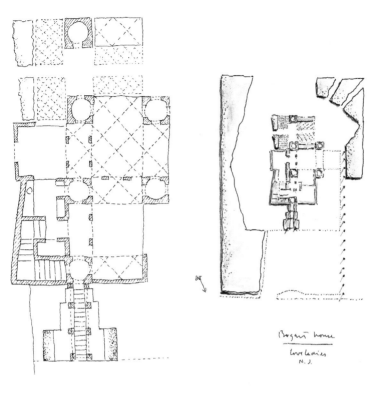

Bogan house
Loveladies
N. J.

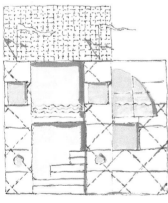

Beach House
Loveladies,
New Jersey

above left
Preliminary
first floor plan
Ink on paper, 1979

above right
Site and first
floor plan
Ink and colored
pencil on paper, 1979

below
South façade
Ink and gouache
on paper, 1979

Castalia, Ministry of Health, Welfare & Sport
The Hague, Netherlands

above
Character studies
Pencil and colored pencil on paper, 1993

below
Character studies
Pencil on yellow tracing paper, 1993

Studies for a hotel in Egypt
Ink on paper, date unknown (1990s)

Denver Central Library
Denver, Colorado
South façade study
Pencil on paper, 1991

1500 Ocean Drive
South Beach, Miami Beach, Florida
Façade study
Pencil on yellow tracing paper, 1993

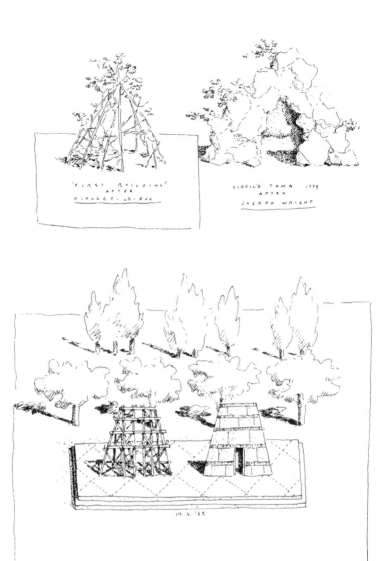

Castelli Leone Folly
New York, New York
Referential sketches, Viollet-le-Duc's
"First Building" (left) and Virgil's
Tomb after Joseph Wright (right)
Ink on paper, 1984

Archaic Vessels for Steuben
Pencil and colored pencil
on yellow tracing paper, 1986

**"Fire" choreographed by Laura
Dean for the Joffrey Ballet**
New York, New York
Costume studies
Ink on paper, 1982

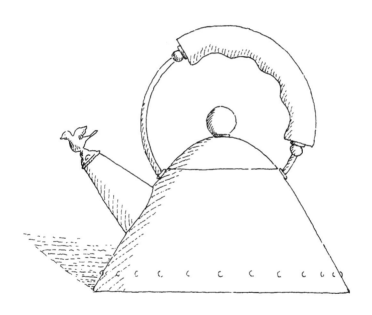

Telling Stories: Character and Context

As Graves describes in his 1977 article on drawing, the design process culminates in a "definitive drawing" that objectively fixes two-and three-dimensional aspects of the composition. Today, this type of drawing is typically produced electronically. However, in much of Graves' work, there is an important intermediate step between the looseness of the preparatory study and the exactitude of the final drawing, a step that develops the character of the building or object in relationship to its context. These drawings, often drawn one over another on yellow tracing paper, explore the final proportions of the architectural composition, and the details, materials and colors that give it unique character. Character studies for a hotel in Egypt, for example, might reflect referential sketches from the region's vernacular architecture, and then be developed into hard-lined and more precise building elevations.

right
Postal and Telecommunication Building
Xiamen, China
West façade study
Pencil and colored pencil on yellow
tracing paper, 1994

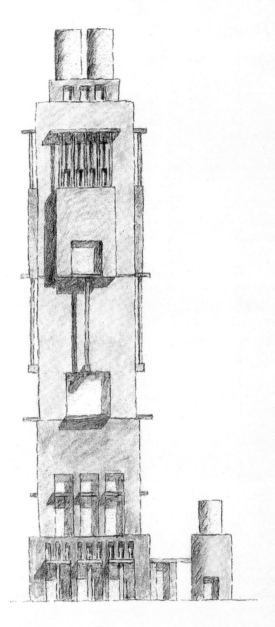

Xiamen Postal
and
Telecommunication
Building

Graves
'94

Michael C. Carlos Museum
Emory University
Atlanta, Georgia
Egyptian Gallery
Ink on paper, 1983

San Juan Capistrano Library
San Juan Capistrano, California
Library entrance from the street
Ink on paper, 1980

Private Residence
Napa Valley, California
Southeast façade study
Pencil and colored pencil on
yellow tracing paper, 1990

Kasumi Research and Training Center
Tsukuba City, Japan
Entrance façade study
Pencil and colored pencil on
yellow tracing paper, 1990

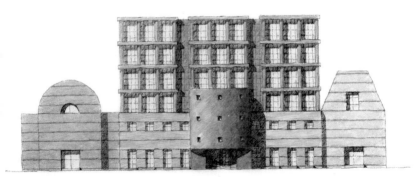

Dining hall facade
Royal Ichikai
hann
1990

above
Royal Ichikai Golf Club
Tochigi Prefecture, Japan
Dining hall façade study
Pencil on yellow tracing paper, 1990

right
Welsh National Center for Literature
Swansea, Wales
Exhibit center lobby
Pencil on paper, 1993

Welsh National Center for Literature

view of lobby

[signature]
'93

above
Saint Martin's College Library
Lacey, Washington
Periodicals reading room
Ink on paper, 1994

left
Nexus Momochi Residential Tower
Fukuoka, Japan
Entrance façade study
Pencil and colored pencil
on yellow tracing paper, 1993

Taiwan Museum of Pre-History
Taitung City, Taiwan
Dining pavilion façade studies
Pencil and colored pencil on yellow
tracing paper, 1993

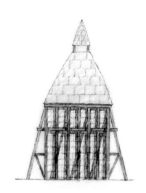

Disney Entertainment Pavilion
Lake Buena Vista, Florida
Walt Disney World
Façade study
Pencil and colored pencil on
yellow tracing paper, 1994

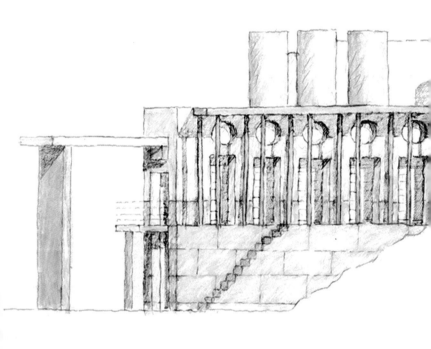

Von Metzsch Residence
Manchester-by-the-Sea, Massachusetts
East façade study
Pencil and colored pencil on
yellow tracing paper, 1994

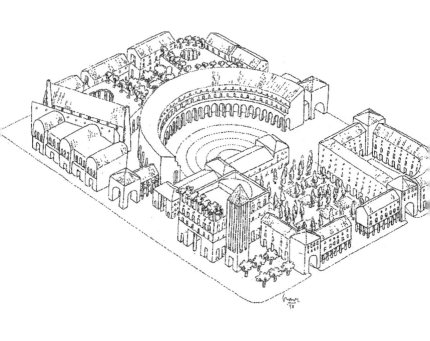

Cosmotoda Master Plan
Barcelona, Spain
Aerial view
Ink on paper, 1998

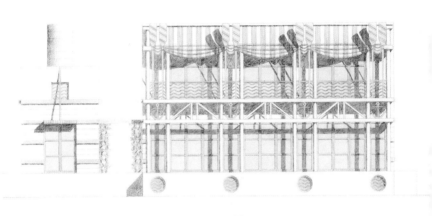

Beach House
Malibu, California
Beach façade study
Pencil and colored pencil
on yellow tracing paper, 1995

Miramar Resort Hotel
El Gouna, Egypt
Character studies
Pencil and colored pencil on
yellow tracing paper, 1995

following pages
Miramar Resort Hotel
El Gouna, Egypt
Main building façade studies
Pencil and colored pencil on yellow
tracing paper, 1995

El Gouna Golf Villas
El Gouna, Egypt
Façade study
Pencil and colored pencil on
yellow tracing paper, 1995

El Gouna Golf Villas
El Gouna, Egypt
Façade study
Pencil and colored pencil on
yellow tracing paper, 1995

above
O'Reilly Theater
Pittsburgh, Pennsylvania
Study for Archaic Landscape mural
Pencil and colored pencil on
yellow tracing paper, 1998

below
St. Mary's Church
Rockledge, Florida
West façade study
Pencil and colored pencil on
yellow tracing paper, 1999

125

Kolonihaven House
Copenhagen, Denmark
Entrance façade
Pencil and colored pencil
on yellow tracing paper, 1996

Kolonihaven House
Copenhagen, Denmark
Side façade
Pencil and colored pencil
on yellow tracing paper, 1996

Phoenix Municipal Government Center
Phoenix, Arizona
Third Street elevation façade
Ink and watercolor on paper, 1985

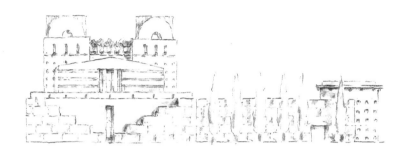

Team Disney Building
Burbank, California
Preliminary façade studies
Pencil and colored pencil on
yellow tracing paper, 1986

Imagined Landscapes

In addition to "Tuscan Landscapes" that recall vernacular buildings and landscape from Graves' many trips to Italy, he has created numerous small gouache paintings that he calls "Archaic Landscapes". These images, which place simple geometric assemblages in an open landscape, serve as a visual diary of compositional ideas. Graves considers the individual figurative elements as primary forms of architecture, fragments that can be incorporated into larger architectural frames.

He uses a similar approach to paintings and Giclée prints made from the paintings to commemorate building openings and other important occasions. For the grand opening of the NCAA Headquarters and Hall of Champions in Indianapolis, Indiana, Graves placed a painting of the NCAA building and representative buildings from the city on an easel sited along a representation of the White River. Local buildings that the Graves firm designed – the headquarters of Thomson Consumer Electronics and the Indianapolis Art Center – occupy the skyline beyond.

Easel Landscape
Pencil and gouache on paper, 1995

Archaic Landscape
Gouache on paper, 1998

**Cover design for
the Roma Interrotta
issue of Architectural
Design (1979)**
Photocopy and gouache
on paper, with paper
photocopy collage, 1978

134

Chiesa de SS Cosma e
Damiano

g. dec Cavalli

GIAMBATTISTA NOLLI

M.G. 78

**NCAA Headquarters and
Hall of Champions**
Indianapolis, Indiana
Commemorative print, Giclée,
(from a painting, pencil and
gouache on paper), 1999

**The Washington Monument
Restoration Washington, D.C.**
Commemorative print, Giclée,
(from a painting, pencil and
gouache on paper), 1999

Tuscan Landscape
Acrylic on canvas, 2011

Biography

Michael Graves, FAIA, has been in the forefront of architecture and design since he founded his practice in 1964. Since then, the practice has evolved into two firms: Michael Graves & Associates, which provides architecture, interior design and master planning services, and Michael Graves Design Group, which specializes in product design, graphic design and branding. The firms are based in Princeton, New Jersey and New York City. Through their multiple studios, the firms are highly integrated and support a continuum among architecture, interiors and furnishings.

The architectural practice has designed over 400 buildings worldwide encompassing many building types: large-scale master plans, corporate headquarters and other office buildings, hotels and resorts, restaurants and retail stores, facilities for sports and recreation, healthcare facilities, civic projects such as embassies, courthouses and monuments, a wide variety of university buildings, museums, theaters and public libraries, housing and single-family residences. From early projects such as the award-winning Humana Building in Louisville, Kentucky, completed in the 1980s, to more recent work such as the Ministry of Health and Sport in The Hague, MGA has directly influenced the transformation of urban architecture from abstract modernism toward more contextual responses. Critic Paul Goldberger, writing in The New York Times, called Graves, "truly the most original voice in American architecture".

The product design practice has designed over 2,000 products, which include a wide variety of consumer products for home, office and personal use, as well as building components such as lighting, hardware, bath and kitchen products. Strategic partnerships have included JCPenney, Target Stores, and manufacturers such as Alessi, Stryker Medical, Steuben, Lenox/Dansk, Disney, Baldinger Architectural Lighting, David Edward Furniture, Delta Faucet, and Progress Lighting among others. MGDG has also designed innovative packaging and graphic identity programs supporting MGDG and MGA projects.

Michael Graves and the firms have received over 250 awards for design excellence. He is the 2012 Richard H. Driehaus Prize Laureate. Graves received the 1999 National Medal of Arts from President Bill Clinton. In 2001, the American Institute of Architects awarded Michael Graves its Gold Medal, the highest award bestowed upon an individual architect. Graves was the recipient of the 2010 AIA/ACSA Topaz Medallion for Excellence in Architectural Education. He was also the first architect inducted into the New Jersey Hall of Fame. In addition, Graves received the inaugural Russel Wright Award for product design, the Tau Sigma Delta Gold Medal, in recognition of his distinguished teaching career, and the William Howard Taft lifetime achievement medal from the University of Cincinnati. He has become internationally recognized as a healthcare design advocate, and in 2010, the Center for Health Design named Michael Graves one of the Top 25 Most Influential People in Healthcare Design. Graves regularly gives lectures to major healthcare advocacy groups, including AARP, the Healthcare Design Conference and TED MED. In March 2013, President Obama appointed Graves to the US Access Board.

A native of Indianapolis, Graves received his architectural training at the University of Cincinnati and Harvard University. In 1960, he won the Rome Prize and studied at the American Academy in Rome for two years, of which he is a Trustee. In 1962, Graves began a 39 year teaching career at Princeton University, where he is now the Robert Schirmer Professor of Architecture, Emeritus. He has received 14 honorary doctorates. He is a member of the National Academy, the American Academy of Arts and Letters and a Fellow of the American Institute of Architects.

Credits

Francesca Serrazanetti
PhD in Architecture, she lectures and
researches at the Architectural Design
Department at the Politecnico di Milano.
She works as independent curator on
exhibitions and publishing projects,
writing on architecture, design and theatre.
She is editor of the magazine 'Stratagemmi'.

Matteo Schubert
Director of the culture department of ABCittà
s.c.r.l. and the architecture firm Alterstudio
Partners srl, with which he has carried
out numerous cultural and architectural
projects for private and public sector clients,
winning national and international awards.
He has developed and curated various events,
exhibitions and publications.

The credits of photographs
reproduced in this volume are:

Pages 142-143
Photographs of Michael Graves
by Marek Bulaj, courtesy of
Michael Graves & Associates.
All others courtesy of Michael
Graves & Associates.